Print information available on the last page

Rev. date: 04/30/2015

To order additional copies of this book, contact:
Xlibris
1-888-795-4274
www.Xlibris.com
Orders@Xlibris.com

Poems from the Village

Rhonda Y. Harrison

Spring

Writers

I was told that writers write daily, and they do
They don't always put pen to paper or press the keys on a computer
But they daydream in every place
Night dream, create in any time and space
The shower is a temple holy
The toilet is a place to kneel and write a prayer
The sink a place to meditate and gaze
Plan the day, week, month, year, if you dare
Yes, plan life away
Creative space
A place of grace
Writers do write daily when the ebb and flow is right
Not forced or pushed and but awake day and night
By thoughts and passions and spirits near and far
That cannot, will not rest until the justice has raised the bar
Dream halted, sentences have been meted
No hate my thoughts have been vetted
I need to see the light and feel the might of a word falling on your heart
See the change it causes when it pierces you like a dart
Heal yourself, ask for forgiveness
Write your own words and story
Cover people in glory
Don't worry what's the use
Be your own muse
Transform to positive from mess
Manifest your progress
Write

A Generation Lost and Found

Let's make quantum leaps
Reclaim
Each one teach one
Retrain
Apply force and agitate
Reestablish face-to-face relationships
Push and pull
Redirect and ease stress
Cause motion with upward gradient velocity
Rebuild
Set positive goals
Realign
Change the trajectory of a generation

Manners

Please and thank you,
What a delight—
A bright smile.
Kneeling and praying for a good night.
Have we gotten away from a lift of a hat, nod of a head, the wave of a cap?
A bow and a curtsy,
A rise from a table,
An opening of the door?
What a shame *no, sir* and *yes, ma'am* aren't used anymore.

Family

People that love each other
My role models
Nana, Mother, Father, Grandmother, Grandfather
Aunts, uncles, cousins
Foster family bonded in love
All of us united, gifts from above
Values, spiritual, generous, and kind
Excel in the classroom but more importantly in life
Beautiful people through and through
Never hesitate to assist and appreciate you
Great cooking, good music, tears, laughter, and dance
Moments to forget and some to cherish
Lessons to learn and grow from
Help families to flourish
Give family a chance

Who Cares

So you think you know what's up and who's really down.
You'll find out when your money and drugs are low or you're wearing a frown
Who shows up for you,
Who really cares,
Who prays for your success and welfare—
Your friends, family, crew, those whom you scare.
Who really cares for you and has your back?
I see your blank stare.
Would you risk your life and mine
For a pull or push of a line?
Would you drop everything
And spend your last dime on a high?
What kind of person risks it all with no reward?
Yes, I see your blank stare.
Whether yellow, white, or black,
If you leave them behind and never look back,
Who will give a crap and really care?

I Am on Happy!

I am on happy!
That's where my dial stays
Most days.

Music Maestro

Music Maestro, play our tune
Our focus is shifted
Our hearts are opened
Our emotions are flowing
Our thoughts are relevant
Moods lifted
Smiles gleaming
Level of consciousness elevated
Encore

Promises

You cannot lie
Every word that you have spoken comes true
A new heaven and a new earth
Skies so blue
Wonderful, bountiful hills, dust and flesh renewed
Youthful bliss, yes, perfection
Refreshed skin, sun kissed
Stars so bright
Moonlit nights
Peace with all animals and humankind
Plenty of grain in every land
Higher thinking from above
A deeper, abounding love
Waters of life, yes, refreshing streams
These are true and solid promises, not just mere dreams

Tall, Dark, and Handsome

Dear Mom
I love who you love
I am watching you
What you tolerate, I do too
What you work hard for, I strive for too
My motivation is yours
My patient attitude of faith comes from you
I will marry my Mr. Tall, Dark, and Handsome soon

Open Heart

Open your heart and let the light shine in
Brighten someone's day
Allow life to begin
At first the concept of love may seem foreign
But an open heart pierces through the soul
Envelops your life force
It allows you and me to love the light and its source

Mirror

Reflecting light,
Image of what I should be.
Adjustments to go from night to daylight,
Truth of greatness in front of me.
Stopped surviving,
Wasting time running away from divine destiny.
What's best for me?
Less stress daily,
Walk toward right and light.
The closer I am to my initiation to paradise,
Imagining growing perfect daily instead of dying,
The sooner I can see the human inside,
The mirror.

Love

Boundless
Matchless
Be sure to find your bliss
Search hard to discover love like this
Laugh till it hurts
Love in action, not just words
My advice is to find your best friend and cling
Like a peach to its pit
When tough times come and they will
Don't be easy to quit
Work hard and build a life together
Continue to flock like birds of a feather
Nothing could be better
Than you, love

BO

Children tell the truth,
You smell bad, look bad.
Don't be so sad,
Just bathe and clean yourself up.
I can help you.
Let me comb your hair,
Brush your teeth, and I'll brush mine too.
Let's gargle minty fresh throats sweet.
I will spray your perfume and put on your high heels.
Where's that fluffy boa and pretty dress?
Where's my shirt and tie?
I'll get you out of this mess.

Not Just for the Birds

Soar above
Fly with me
No drugs needed
Just faith in your own wings

Fall

My Heart Weeps for You

To watch the pain and ravages of HIV and AIDS
And yet I don't really know you
To be loved by my adopted parents
And yet I can't touch you
To see the love and concern in a stranger's eyes
And yet I can't hold you
Dear Mother, I long to see your face
Hear and see your graceful walk in my space
I did not ask to come to this place
Please, God, grant me the will to keep up this pace
My legacy is lost and yet it is beginning again with me
Give me Your will to see how I may honor Thee
Never to repeat what's been done to me
Born into sudden death and lost without a chance to dance
Or truly be free
I will never procreate
To do so would seal my child's fate
Death knocking at their door
A life without hope once more

Absence

They say that absence makes the heart grow fonder
I don't believe this to be true
When you promise to show and never do
I don't feel any closer to you
They say that a little space will draw you closer
I don't believe this to be true
Memories of your back and not your face haunt my door
Money and presents can never replace your presence, your face
I need much more
Time is precious, and yet we all have the same allotted each day
What you choose to do with yours is to go your own way
I guess I can forgive you and myself
But I cannot forget
The feelings that I carry with me in my head and heart
Are to be a better person and never regret
We will all be absent for a short while
Just mere dust again in a pile

The Best Is Yet Be

I know your name
Lonely existence in a distant space
Living in disgrace and shame in your mind
Let the world see the true you
Reconcile yourself
Outside of the closet door of fear
We love you still
The family bond is real
With your heart of magnolia steel
Heighten our thought continuum
The world's a different place
Show your real face
Set all things free
No inhibitions
The best is yet be

Pain, Anguish, and Fear

Pain, anguish, and fear
All signs to me that a breakthrough is near
I'm not breaking down
I am breaking through to a life that parallels truth
Opposite of this dark world
On the path to life, so don't pull me down or knock me over
Pull me up and work with me on your shoulder
I'll carry your burdens and you carry mine
We'll pray together and leave them with Thine
The promises to allay our fears and dry our tears
Are real for the one who peers
Into the Word and lives boldly
Despite trials causing pain, anguish, and fear

Fear vs. Faith

Faith interrupted
Ending dreams abruptly
Annihilation of self
Reasons not to challenge the status quo
Verses

Fullness of life,
Answers from above,
Intimate talks with God,
Trusting completely in love,
Hope founded in truth.

No Time for Drama

Dear person out there in the universe,
I apologize that you feel some kind of way about me,
But I don't have time to conspire against you.
I am too worried about keeping me and mine on the road to everlasting life
And keeping my stuff straight in this life.
I have little or no time for drama,
Peace.

Summer

The Glider

We glide
We fan and sweat
And pray for a cool summer breeze
We sip a cup of sweet tea
Hold a Mason jar of ice water
Or even a Pepsi bottle
A brief hello from a passerby
A deep talk with friends
Or a lullaby
Big, full hips swaying from side to side
Cars beep and people shout sweet melodies while going to and fro
Comforting and feeding souls as they walk by
A few dollars' worth of bologna or minced ham from Johnson's corner store
I didn't know that you could order by the pound for several years more
Sweet memories of childhood waiting for the aunts and uncles to walk through the door
Waiting for the mailman, milkman, farmer, fisherman, and insurance man's lure
Selling burial plots and collecting money galore
That's all the security and land that we can own or afford
A squeak and a sigh
A shoo, whoota-toota-mae
A dash for the bathroom
Catch the door and kill that fly
Peaceful moments of the day and tension reliever
Swing and glide the cares of the day away
You make me a believer
A new blessing to count each and every day

Mother

My first love
Superhero
Lover of people
Nurturer of souls
Feeder of dreams
Listener of stories
Speaker of legends
Dinner-maker and educator
Passer of the torch of light
Gentle nature
Fighter
Yes, Mother

Her Story Is History

Black woman
West Virginian mountain momma
Native American, deeply rooted
Ghetto child
New Jersey suburban Nubian queen
Ohio summers and Virginia Beach bum
Pennsylvania, New York, Boston dreamer
Speak proper, Valley girl
Teen mom
Love people, too trusting
Hurt, bruised, damaged
Stripped, drugged, raped, naked
Hired and fired
Loved and hated
Accosted, abandoned, left for dead, aborted mission
Forgetting is a protection from painful memories
Shedding the guilt and shame
Cried, prayed, repented, healed, released
Loved back to health
Made whole
Rich, forgiven, restored, truly blessed beyond imagination

I

I was put here to make you laugh
I was sent to use my rod and staff
I was brought here to make you cry
I was sent here to make you live, not die
I was called here to make you fly
I am not here for the status quo
I am here to make things better
Now try

The Eye

The eye, the window to your soul
When you see it, you admire it
You desire it
You conspire to get it
You require it and burn on fire for it
Live in debauchery and mire for it
Become a liar for it
Watch what you watch

Amish

Plain but not so simple
Isolated but not closed off
Forgiving but never forgetting
Sheltered but not protected
Dark but enlightened
Faithful and prayerful
Simple yet so complex
Hungry and yet so full
Sowers of seed and harvesters of good
Potential beyond measure

Fire

Be on fire
Live on purpose
Strike a balance
Love and lift people up
Encourage their dreams
Conquer
You will follow in the rise from the ashes

Track

Practice, focus, and see the goal
Stay loose and warm up
Ready, set, gun, start, and I'm off
In the zone, blurred faces, clear vision, muffled cheers
Cold baton, hug the curves and white lines
Controlled breathing and hit stride
Ignore the pain, push through, and finish strong
Lean forward and cross the finish line first
Team player, acclaim, affirmation
Perseverance, practice, and meditation paid off

Beautiful Breed

Skin black, white, golden, or brown
I smile as I see your curly locks and straight braids hanging down
Close shaven or bald head
Smiles not ever ceasing, never dead
Beautiful souls all around
Sun-kissed skin
White boy grin
Black and brown
Dimples in cheeks and chin
Beauty within
Blessing the world
My beautiful boy and girl
Greatness is calling you

Brothers and Sisters

Family for days
Where "a little one will become a thousand"
A reflection of God
Smiles and genuine ties
Where true fellowship lies
Wholeness and honesty
Strengths meet weaknesses
And power is given
Cleanliness and trueness
Paradise

Raft

Be like a raft
Explore the world
Carry your messages away
Love, listen, learn, and pray
Teach, train, and transform
Live in the moment today
Excel and be well
Just to dwell in a space in someone's heart
For a spell

Commanded to Love

Help the weaker ones
Aid the poor, widow, and orphans
Be compassionate and forgiving
Be generous and merciful
Be hospitable and kind
What you give to the world is what you get

Beauty All Around

Look up instead of looking down,
Take in the beauty all around;
Did it all happen by chance?
Go ahead, take a breath and another glance.
You are a miracle,
And I too, I must admit,
Although the shoe may not seem to fit.
Whether you've been natured or nurtured to maturity,
It is pretty undeniable and very evident on a clear, starlit night
To perceive His awesome power, glory, love, and might.
We humans are very small, of this there is no doubt.
Thankfully, You are a just God, true and all about.
In the warmth of the sun,
As a new day has begun,
We feel Your glow all around.
In the extreme Alaska cold
And in the brilliance of the old,
Your wisdom, unmatchable, is all around.
Creation's songs teaming with joy resound;
If we release our ego
And really let go,
We can attain to live forever
And be aligned with true purpose and Thee.

You Are

You are that song in my head that brings back summer love
You are that scent in my bed that makes me sigh
You are the beautiful sunset that makes me smile
You have a sweet, tender kiss that gives me butterflies
You have that perfect touch that covers me with love
I can see, hear, smell, feel, and taste you
You bring me right back to that time and space of love

Winter

The Most Powerful Weapons

My pen is my weapon of choice
Peace is the key
Yeah, the gauntlet has been thrown
We can change more lives by studying the Good Book

Liar

You'd rather tell a lie than speak the truth
Hide away from the hurt
Get away with something wrong
To get your own way
Selfish stabs at the world
Shout out in fear
Fifty names to fit in
Tons of friends to cover loneliness
Be your own hero
Find your own truth
Get out of the lying mess
Find the true authentic you

Cracks

What leads to divorce?
Not you, beautiful child;
It's the flaws in us big people,
The cracked and broken hearts unrestored.
It's the cracks causing damaged trust
And empty spaces undefended,
Dividing us, thoughts and dreams unbending,
The hopes of our family unattended to.
Not you, not our love,
It's the cracks.

Bullies Come in All Sizes

Bullies come in all sizes, shapes, and colors
Some big, some small, some short, and some tall
Bullies show up in the strangest places
At school, church, the park, and, on the job
It's just not cool
They are from all races and faces
It's hard to erase them
Now that they are in your head
And filling it with dread
I know I've been on both sides of this fence
You've built up a wall
It's a perfect defense
They come in all age groups, you know
Once you've beat off one, another shows
You say a prayer, forgive them and yourself
And hope that they will flee
But nothing seems to make them let you be free
Enslaved by their taunts
The shy, bright star that you are is dimmed
The problem is not with you, though
They just can't see the beauty and uniqueness in you
It's their loss, not yours
They need to hurt others to feel better, of course
While you try to help others
They can't justify destroying lives and declining help
While your awesome self is undeniably felt
Don't give up even if they don't see
I know and you know that all you need is to be
Be free
Say I can be authentically me
Authentically me daily

Forgiveness Denied

I forgive you
Nah, I don't need it
You see, the thing is that this forgiveness is for me
And not for you only
I need to heal and feel better
If for a moment
Yeah, so accept it or not
It's your choice
But I choose to forgive you
Because it's the only way that I can forget
And move forward

What Is Love?

Love is allowing yourself to be loved
Love is a progression from eros
Love is being open and full of Philadelphia
Love is acknowledging a boundless capacity within you
Love is to embrace the world and change it
Love is seeing true agape staring you in the face daily
Love is being man or woman enough to allow yourself to be wronged
Love is making sacrifices and compromises without regret
Love is giving more and never expecting a thing in return
Love is embracing the unloved, uncaring, hurt souls who cannot love themselves
Love pursues peace and chases after kindness
Love is gracious and patient with others
Love is your brand

Homesick

Remembering the sights and the sounds
Sand on the streets and loud beats playing
Corner singing and children laughing and playing
Walking uptown and to the park
At church singing and studying day and night
Conferences, cakes, the smell of cookies and pies
Ski-jogging on snow-filled streets
Snowball fights and hitchhiker bites
Playing freeze tag and jumping double dutch
Hopscotch and hide-and-seek
Dodgeball and kickball in the street
Football and baseball at the field
House parties and Hong Hing treats
Field Day at Berkeley and swimming at night
Roller-skating and running till dusk
Modelling, PVH, and Emerson walks to work
College commuter, learning to drive
Catching the 165, 11A, and 11C
For NYC Red and Tan and NJ transit were a must
Making new friends and keeping some old
Growing up in a safe place made us bold
Bear Mountain, Spring Valley, and the Nyack Waterfront
Yankees games, Knicks and Mets and Nets too
Hat day, bat day, mug day, anything new
Girl Scouts camping and singing
Running track and winning
Garden and Danbury State Fairs
Vernon Valley, Great Gorge
Six Flags and Madison Square Garden
Rye Playland, Long Island, and Staten Island too
Newark Symphony Hall and Broadway, what a hoot
Yes, sometimes I long to see you and recall way back when
Things were much simpler then . . . yeah, I'm home sick again

They Are All Our Children

Every parent wants what is best for their children
Your duty is to be honest and love unconditionally
Respect is earned
Obedience is owed
Mutual appreciation, it often grows
Open communication must be nurtured
You don't have to tell all, but not all secrets are good
Protection and shelter are promised
Unguard your hearts for things go well
Receive the message
Parents can discern the danger around corners
Yield to love and discover your path
Live fast, die young is a lie that Satan tells
Eve was fooled, and Adam didn't fare well
Life everlasting is much more rewarding
Our hope for all children is that the "celestial chariot" you will be boarding

Survivor's Guilt

I inhale as you take your last breath;
Now you are forever with me.
Why ask why when only more questions seem to come?
Tears never ceasing,
Pain never easing.
I still see your face;
Now I'm chasing your dreams and mine.
I try to clearly define and walk the line
Awake but I want to be asleep.
Take my breath away,
Getting faded to escape,
Try to talk and walk through it with grace.
I can't erase the pain and the survivor's guilt I face—
Missing you.

Unfaithful

Double life connections
Emotional scars running deep
Cuts deeper than the ocean
Sworn to silence
Secrets between two and God
Jeopardizing family
Putting our innocent lives at risk
Down low actions of lust
Selfish flesh and lies
Sword-fighting behavior in cover of night
Slay your demons and I'll battle mine
Denial and more betrayal
Never forget intuition
The gut doesn't lie
Hurt feelings, lost intimacy, and poor health
Feel real love
Have a "come to Muhammad, Buddha, or Jesus" moment
Take whatever time that you need
Think and be decisive
It's a slippery slope in this life that you lead
Know the truth of a touch
Be honest and heal yourself
Rebuild emotional love
Make a decision
Go left or right
Forgiveness exists despite your negligent paths
We are all a ball of contradictions
We all make mistakes
Now clean up your mess
Unfaithful

Venom

Do you conjure up that venom especially for me?
Do you treat every perceived threat with such contempt?
Love taps from Satan,
No thanks.
Should I "heap fiery coals upon your head" until the icicles melt from your heart?
Should I kill you with kindness,
Snuff you out with silence,
Or use my words to conquer you for good?
Venomous creature . . . oh no, misunderstood.

Marked for Death

Put down the gun and take a deep breath.
Survival of the fittest, is that all that's left?
Is it really kill or be killed
In this life, dear?
Be ready to hustle and play in the game.
Careful, I'm spitting bullets with my tongue
And shooting arrows just the same.
No, I'm not Katniss or GI Jane,
Breaking down walls with words,
Trampling on strife,
Words are my weapon of choice.
Speak up, rap on, use your God-given voice.
Do not fear censorship,
Just speak your mind,
Don't fear the grind;
Haunted by night and day,
Chased by verbs,
Pursued by subject till thoughts and dreams align.
Convey your own rift,
Make a shift,
We all have innate talent;
Tap into it and flow it freely from your palate,
Channel it,
Fuse it, light it up,
The battle is with yourself; we all fall short, live too little.
You're marked for death if you fail to really live,
Use your gifts.

The Life of a Slave

Poor and black
Born into circumstance
Change slow
No rights
No worries, no problems
No planning for a brighter tomorrow
No plight greater
No flight left
Hoping for death and a better life
My family is long gone
Just myself alone to weep
Memories of smiling faces who have gone to sleep
Pray and sing and pray some more
Till my tired bones fall fast asleep
Wake up early and back to work
Field or house related to the same task
Sing freedom songs
Learn to read and write
Don't let the word out
Hide the books in the board in the floor
Just in case someone knocks on the wooden house door
Domestic's busy, musicians and field workers too
Waiting on freedom, raped, longing for their just due
Look up to the North Star, follow the riverbanks, and across to freedom we go
Look for friends and quilts
Living hand to mouth and accepting generosity
Singing songs of freedom till my dying day
Then I'll rest with Thee

Equality

Despite our feeble efforts, we are not color-blind.
Many open doors
Have just as rapidly been closed.
Inequality and a racial divide still exist:
Sneezing the N-word, whistling Dixie, and hocking
spit in front of women, fraternity chants,
Outright hate and codes of disrespect.
Tracks, streets, and invisible barriers separate us,
Joblessness and unemployment,
Dumbing ourselves down—
Why?
From the wrong side of the tracks,
But who says you have to remain?
We may be black and poor, but is that the status
only to maintain?
Some say pockets of successful blacks exist,
Even some upper crust and elite thrive,
While many of us see black men without apparent
reason die.
Segregation is still commonplace today,
Sad but true.
The increasing economic divide has become a rule,
Just look at your own church, cafeteria, college
campus, or beehive,
Comfort in the safe zone of friendly faces that look
like yours and mine.
Just as the *Birth of a Nation* hurt us,
This great economic rift does fine;

Are you so *Gone with the Wind* that you forgot that
we are all created equal?
Heighten your awareness,
Raise your mind;
Systemic issues of poor housing, blatant prejudice
in employment, and inadequate education
Stem from hate,
So shine a light.
Beyond white guilty minds, we need real
conversations,
Strong individual family units and leaders,
Honest analysis to combat this plight,
Early childhood education programs of
accountability,
Inclusion and love to win this fight,
Reversal of discriminatory prison sentencing,
Affirmative action and restoration—
Reparation statutes at the federal level will be a
good start.
Let's talk real solutions,
Be a part, because equality starts in the heart.
Choose a road, choose life and light;
True equality can only come through God's
righteous kingdom might.
Don't sit idle,
Stay and pray,
Dare to stand for what is just and right.

I Was Made to Love You Too

While you were sleeping
I was steady creeping
I love you too
But you can't compare to boo
You sympathize and me you legitimize
You rock my world and me you mesmerize
But I do love being with another
He just happens to be my brother
He knows how to touch me where you won't dare go
He knows how to reach in and pull out my soul
I was just experimenting and fell deeply in love
It's not my first love affair of this caliber
The world won't open up to let me face that fact
Especially being Hispanic, Muslim, and black
No, I'm not on the down low
I figured that you had to know
The late-night calls and talks
The long, intimate private walks
The drinks by the pool and nights on the beach
I know you are not blind
You kept your cool
You couldn't bear to see
Because I was made to love you two
Yes the both of you

Don't Be Amazed

Don't chastise me about my chains
When you put them on me,
Don't define me by my deficiencies
When your generosity is short,
Don't stare at my scars and scoff
When you're the one giving the lashes,
Don't fortuitously acknowledge my fear
When you perpetrate the torture,
Don't be perplexed by my pain
When you are the one that turned up the flames of persecution,
Don't expect me to always be kind
When your sweet delivery is bitter inside,
Don't put my rhymes down
When you created my jungle streets, winding road, and heavy load,
Don't close your ears to my voice and my melody
When you have no song and sing off-key,
Don't be a hater and expect peace
When you have failed to love and are at war,
Don't be amazed
When the world that you claim to be the center of, that magically appeared,
Turns on you and demands accountability,
Don't be amazed
When you lead me to quicksand, I decided to keep my head and hand upward,
Don't be surprised
When I decide to rise up,
Take hold of the outstretched hand of my people that rescued me, instead of waiting for you.

You give me the words

You give me life
You give me the words to write
When I've lost my will and might
You take corrective action to love me and make things right
A brain among nerds
Yet at a loss for words
When I'm brought before kings
You give me the words to say and sing
To testify about your healing power
To continue serving you with honor in that hour
To declare your great and holy name
I'm left to contemplate faith and fame
Why was I given life?
Why was I spared?
Why was the good news with me shared?
Have I lived up to my true calling and potential grand?
To be able before you, to stand
To raise your mind and game
You cannot remain the same
You were chosen from a few
To lead a family and a nation beyond what you once knew
Keep giving us the words to live by

Ryan's Song

Twenty-two reigns forever,
Ryan was that clever;
Geniuses never have long lives,
But they have great impact,
Never forget that.
Memories on your mind, wristband, tattoo,
A work of art—
The joy and pain will pierce all
Straight to the heart.

I'll be there where my image stays;
"Kiss, Ryan, Adam/Jason," Eric prays.
My gram said that I played in her hair the night I passed,
Now I'm forever in her head, always a blast from the past.
My dancing feet never stopped making people laugh;
You can take my life but the joy that I have brought lasts.
Didn't you know like my family knows?
"That HRS, Henry's Run Shit"—Thanks, Renee.

Now you must do the heavy lifting,
For I have chopped down trees and blazed the trails,
Especially for my parents, friends, teammates, cousins, and siblings,
Charting the way to success,
Conquering challenges and winning many victories together.

My life was too short but, certainly full of impact.
I'm smiling and crying now,
Learning to trust my wings,
Living to be happy and fully filled with peace as you live.

This song will never end,
There will always be another beautiful facet of me to write about in
"Ryan's Song."

I have elevated the lives and minds of dear Destiny and others, "Angel of Mine."
I left many to mourn and celebrate my short life.
A friend ponders and writes, "Two friends separated by miles yet still connected. We each lost our sons a day apart from each other. We laid them to rest on the same day. Dina, our hearts were heavy for our own sons and our dear friend's. Many miles separated us, and yet we are so close. They are forever in my heart." —Aquansa
"I wish, I wish, I wish. I wish, I wish, I wish."
"After all my strength is gone. I look to you."

Tomorrow's not promised, and today's just a gift.
"I bought a charm for Brandon, he wears it every day so you are always close to his heart. We miss you so much. It's hard to believe one person touched so many hearts, but you did. I see the messages people write, and I stop to think how lucky I was to have known you. How lucky I was to have seen you that day. How lucky I was that you got to see our on, your godson, that very day you left this earth. I know you are always watching over him. Thank you. You will *always* hold a special place in my heart. My son will always know who you are and how much you loved life. We love you, Jerz. Until we meet again, xoxo." —Sheena Sowers

"My nephew, the light and love of my being. Who challenged and defeated all obstacles placed in your path. When society counted you out you knew that you would excel to heights only you knew were possible. In the 25yrs God loaned us you he showed us that greatness could not be defined, that love could not be contained and that hard work and determination separates the weak from the strong. So Ryan, with your crooked smile, confidence and swagger for days keep banging your head and keep protecting and cloaking us for all our days until we meet you and Dina again. My hero." —Aunt Rosalyn

Always something there to remind me of how great you are,
So many sacrifices that you made to enable us to live,
To stand up, our spirit caress,
Picking up the pieces of my broken heart and mess;
You make me stronger and yet afraid to love harder.

Life, too short but certainly full of impact;
I'm smiling and crying,
Learning to trust my wings as you did, Ryan,
Living to be happy and fully filled with peace as you lived.
This song will never end;
There will always be another beautiful facet of you to write about in
"Ryan's Song."

The blossoming of a friendship is rare, true, and amazing gift beyond compare.
Genesis 4:9–16, "We should all be our brother's keeper."
I will never be ready to say good-bye to such a sweet soul . . . Ryan, I love you, and you knew that! At
age three you had more common sense than most adults.
Jehovah is a god of justice, wisdom, power, and most of all, love;
He will do what needs to be done in His own timetable.
Until then, may my tears water the seeds of love that I plant and yield results.
See you in the resurrection. You are always on my mind and in my heart, nephew.
The world only saw a glimpse of the light that you had to shine,
"Candle in the wind!" Love, Aunt Rhonda.
Life, too short but certainly full of impact,
I'm smiling and crying now,
Learning to trust my wings as you did,
Living to be happy and fully filled with peace as you lived,
This song will never end,
There will always be another beautiful facet of you to write about in
"Ryan's Song."

Ryan "Jerz" Henry 4/22/1986–9/4/2011
Truly one of a kind.

(Negatives)

written by Stephanie Guzman

I kept rearranging the pictures on the wall. I was obsessed with having all the corners straight. After a couple of hours, I stepped back and observed the final product. My dorm room was finally complete. Almost immediately, I pulled out my cellphone and took pictures of my room to send to my sister and mom but then stopped. I stood in front of the pictures I just finished arranging and stared at each one individually—not a single picture from my childhood. I sent the pictures of my finished room to my family as I lay in bed; my mind became fixated on the lack of childhood pictures. I attempted to redirect my mind and get mentally prepared for the start of my first semester away from home, but that was interrupted with the flooding of memories not pictured. The truth of the matter is very few of my childhood pictures existed because a camera and film did not fit into the family budget. I lay in bed that night thinking about the memories not recorded on my wall. Pictures of days that now seem so distant but were the sole motive I pressed onto college; the days when the struggles of growing up in a single-parent household were shadowed in bitter happiness.

Students laughing in the hallway keep me up. I toss and turn in bed attempting to fall asleep in disbelief that I am here. Yes, I am a college student, but I finally have a room of my own.

I remember Christmas before we moved into our first home. Before that, the three of us were crammed into a small attic apartment, so the Christmas tree was miniature. Light cascading from the narrow attic window illuminated the tinfoil base of the tree during the day. It sat with tiny pendants chaotically glued on every branch. Now when I see these trees, they are typically a centerpiece on tables. During this merry season, however, it stood six feet tall to my eyes, like any Christmas tree to a child. That tree sat by the small attic window for years during Christmas time, and I always picked it up to admire the glitter and small details that vanished over time. With the excitement of unwrapping gifts, Jazmin and I forgot that today was important for another reason too.

We turned and began singing "Happy Birthday" to our mom, and she just hugged us. Her birthday was on Christmas, and these two young girls had nothing to give her for years. This birthday had gone unrecognized for a long time, but I was six and now comprehended it was also her day. All those years, it had been overlooked yet she never let it disturb her, handing over presents and glowing as she watched her children freak out. There are no accounts on film of Christmas at that apartment on King Street. More unsettling, there were no pictures of my mom with even a birthday cake.

I turn on my television hopeful it would help my restlessness depart. Of course, my favorite episode of SpongeBob is on, the Halloween special.

My friends always showed me photographs of their childhood Halloween costumes. I just remember the time when I wanted to be the pink Power Ranger. I continued my attitude until we got to the Crispus Attucks Community Center for a Halloween bash. Once I was there, I was finally satisfied with my Esmeralda costume and running about with my friends and sister. Finally, being here wasn't annoying. Jazmin and I were there every day for the after-school program. After the program was over, Jazmin and I went downstairs to the basement where a homeless shelter was located and where my mom worked. We stayed there until she got off of work. Occasionally, we slept in Ms. Bobbie's office and woke up in our beds at home. I hated the smell of the basement; it always smelled of must but I was never to comment on it. People with dingy clothes and huge backpacks always filed in, and I became familiar with them. Now I was upstairs, enjoying time with friends and not dreading the long night ahead. I bet my mom was too, dressed as a pumpkin, conversing with coworkers. Man, I wish there was a picture of her in that ridiculous costume.

Maybe I need something to drink? I sit the glass of water on my nightstand next to a photograph of my grandmother. I know she would be proud of me.

Memories of our last months with our grandmother, my *abuela*, do not exist but still flash back to me from time to time in a dreary black-and-white. My mom was her caretaker—managing two pre-teen daughters, fresh out of a breakup and now caring for her ill mother. I rarely saw my mom during those couple of months as she went nights without coming home. Jazmin and I were in charge of our own maintenance during that time. We routinely went over to our *abuela's* house after school every day. Seeing her week to week deteriorate into nothing was hard. I didn't fully understand that she was going to die even when my mom came home on a cold, Friday night and explained to us that she would be transported from Hospice to home. She told us they were taking out her feeding tube, and in that moment I realized she was going to be leaving this earth. And she was going to do it by starving herself to death.

I held my mom as she cried for nights after the passing of my *abuela*. I was only ten. Going through albums, I rarely find pictures of us with our grandma and even less of my mom with her mom.

I guess I desired the pictures more for my mom than I did for myself. She was the piece that was missing in my collection. Reoccurring images of my friends were plastered on my wall, yet few with the person who didn't allow self-pity, regardless of my circumstances. I now record these memories in my writing by preserving them as ink on paper: my "photographs." Perhaps the lack pictures was a good thing.

It is true; pictures show you how things were physically. However, a simple photo cannot encapsulate emotions.

Those photos hung on my wall as decoration but became a symbol for me, particularly the pictures that weren't there-- the negatives.

References for "Ryan's Song"

Thanks to all the people who contributed to "Ryan's Song" (Diane, Eric, Destiny, Aquansa, Renee, Sheena and Rosalyn).

Rhett Lawrence and Travon Potts, "Angel of Mine," 1997.

Genesis 4:9–16, "We should all be our brother's keeper."
The New World Translation of the Holy Scriptures (NWT), 2013.

Isaiah 60:22, "The little one will become a thousand and the small one a mighty nation. I myself, Jehovah will speed it up in its own time."
The New World Translation of the Holy Scriptures (NWT), 2013.

"I wish, I wish, I wish. I wish, I wish, I wish." —R. Kelly
"After all my strength is gone. I look to you." —Whitney Houston, written by R. Kelly

R. Kelly. *I Wish*. "I Wish," compact disc. 2000.
Whitney Houston, written by R. Kelly. "I Look to You," compact disc. 2009.

Romans 12:19–20, "Do not avenge yourselves, beloved, but yield place to the wrath; for it is written: 'Vengeance is mine; I will repay,' says Jehovah.' But 'if your enemy is hungry, feed him; if he is thirsty, give him something to drink; for by doing this you will heap fiery coals on his head.' Do not let yourself be conquered by the evil, but keep conquering the evil with the good."
The New World Translation of the Holy Scriptures (NWT) 2013.

"It takes a whole village to raise a child." —African Proverb **http://www.worldofproverbs. com/2012/04/it-takes-whole-village-to-raise-child.html**

Index

RHONDA Y. HARRISON, MBA

Rhonda is an advocate and guardian of one of our most precious assets, our children and the community or village in which they are raised. Whether with her family, as an accounting manager at Community First Fund in Lancaster, Pennsylvania, at her Kingdom Hall, or in volunteer work, she understands that our children are the future of our global village. As a teacher, she is driven by her values and the need to connect children to their heritage and history. She is an exceptional communicator, and in fact, her poems are an outpouring of her work to teach her own children the power of reading and education. Rhonda holds a master of business administration degree from Elizabethtown College. This is her first published project. She is one of Jehovah's Witnesses. She is married to a loving husband of twenty-three and a half years and has three beautiful children, a daughter-in-law, and four lovely grandchildren. Rhonda enjoys music, reading, traveling, and storytelling. Her venture, Reach Your Heights (RYH), aims to advocate for all nationalities to reach their full potential in business, reading, writing, and the arts.

Rhonda's family stressed the importance of family unity, education, giving back to the community, and most of all, love of God. Her "village," the Cox, Washington, Allen, Mason, Stewart, Price, Green, Brown and Harrison families, believes in nurturing all of God's children. Thus, they are living out the old African proverb that "it takes a whole village to raise a child." The loss of many dear loved ones has motivated Rhonda to publish her work now. Rhonda hopes that you enjoy reading *Poems from the Village*, a gift from her heart to yours. Please share them with your friends and family. Future projects include *Short Stories and Novels from the Village*.

Edwards Brothers Malloy
Thorofare, NJ USA
May 18, 2015